STUDY BOOKS

GENERAL EDITOR: RAY MITCHELL, BA
Teaching Adviser to East Suffolk Education Authority

AIRCRAFT by R. J. Pattle
BRIDGES by David Bingley
CANALS by Geoffrey Middleton
CHURCHES by Clifford Warburton
COAL by Eric Baxter
FARMING by Clifford Warburton
THE FIRE SERVICE by Rowland W. Purton
FOODS by Ella Northfield
GAS by Eric Baxter
HOUSES by Clifford Warburton
LAMPS AND CANDLES by Ray Mitchell
THE LAND by Ronald S. Barker
MAPS by Ronald S. Barker
MARKETS by Ronald S. Barker
MONEY by Ronald S. Barker
OIL by Eric Baxter
PAPER by Clifford Warburton
POWER by Clifford Warburton
PRINTING by John Ryder
RADIO by Geoffrey Middleton
RAILWAYS by Eric Baxter
ROADS by Geoffrey Middleton
SAFETY AT SEA by Eric Baxter
SHIPS by Eric Baxter
TELEGRAPHS by Ray Mitchell
TIME AND CLOCKS by A. H. Naylor
WATER SUPPLY by Eric Baxter
WEATHER by Ronald S. Barker

ISBN 0 370 00822 7
Printed Offset Litho and bound in Great Britain for
The Bodley Head Ltd
9 Bow Street, London WC2E 7AL
by Cox & Wyman Ltd, Fakenham
Set in Monotype Plantin
First published 1961
Reprinted 1968, 1972

THE STUDY BOOK OF

CANALS

BY GEOFFREY MIDDLETON

DRAWINGS BY

HEATHER COPLEY

FIRST CANAL OFFICE BIRMINGHAM

THE BODLEY HEAD

LONDON SYDNEY TORONTO

CONTENTS

WOODEN DRAWBRIDGE OVER CANAL

☆ **A canal is a waterway which has been built by man.**

It is used to carry goods in boats from one place to another.

THE FIRST CANALS

☆ The Egyptians, the Assyrians and the Chinese were building canals as long ago as five hundred years before Jesus was born.

Some were used to carry goods, but others were built to drain the water from the land.

One of the most famous early canals was the Grand Canal in China. It took hundreds of years to build and was many hundreds of miles long.

The Romans built many canals throughout their large Empire. In Britain they built the Foss Dyke from Lincoln to the River Trent.

From about 1300 onwards, many other canals were built throughout Europe.

THE GRAND CANAL TODAY

THE GREAT CANAL AGE IN ENGLAND

☆ Just over two hundred years ago there were no railways, there were no aircraft, and the roads were bad.

Horses pulled heavily laden wagons along the rough roads, which were little more than muddy tracks with deep ruts and potholes. When it rained the ruts filled with mud, in which the wagons stuck.

Goods were also carried in large bundles on horses, called packhorses. Often there was no room for a man to ride on them. He had to walk behind.

Many years before, boats had carried goods up the rivers to the inland towns, but now there were long stretches where the rivers could not be used. The boats were bigger and many rivers had filled up with mud. So quicker and cheaper means of transport had to be found.

At this time the Duke of Bridgewater had a coalmine on his estate at Worsley, about seven miles from Manchester. The coal had to be sent by packhorse. Only a small amount could be carried at a time and the journey was slow.

The Duke decided to build a canal from his mine to Manchester, for he knew he could carry more coal on a boat than on horses. It would cost less to send it and the price of coal could be reduced.

He obtained permission by Act of Parliament to construct his canal in 1759, and he employed an engineer called James Brindley to build it.

CANAL ENTERING WORSLEY COALMINE

James Brindley was a farmer's son who was born in Derbyshire in 1716. He had little education and could only write his name and do very simple sums.

He worked on his father's farm until he was 17, but was not very happy there. He wanted to make things so he left the farm and became an apprentice at a foundry. When he was 26, he started his own business as an engineer.

It took Brindley two years to build the canal from Worsley to Manchester. It was about ten miles long.

When building the Duke's canal, Brindley decided to take it over the River Irwell. No one had ever done such a thing before and people laughed at the idea. However, he built a special bridge to carry the water over the river at Barton. Such a bridge is called an *aqueduct*.

The Duke of Bridgewater extended his canal to Runcorn on the River Mersey and so joined it up with the port of Liverpool. Then coal could be taken to the large ships at the docks and goods could be brought from the docks to the towns by boats on the canals.

DUKE OF BRIDGEWATER AT BARTON AQUEDUCT

Brindley was now in great demand. He linked up industrial towns in the Midlands with the rivers Mersey and Trent by building the Grand Trunk Canal. Other canals connected the Midlands with the rivers Severn and Thames. Birmingham became an important industrial centre. The canals carried raw materials for factories, and the goods made there, about the country more cheaply and easily than ever before.

Brindley had built a system of inland waterways when it was urgently needed. He is often called the "Father of British Canals".

Later, in 1793, work commenced on the Grand Junction Canal. This ran from Brentford on the Thames to Braunston in Northamptonshire, and joined up with other canals to Birmingham and the Midlands. Today it is part of the Grand Union Canal.

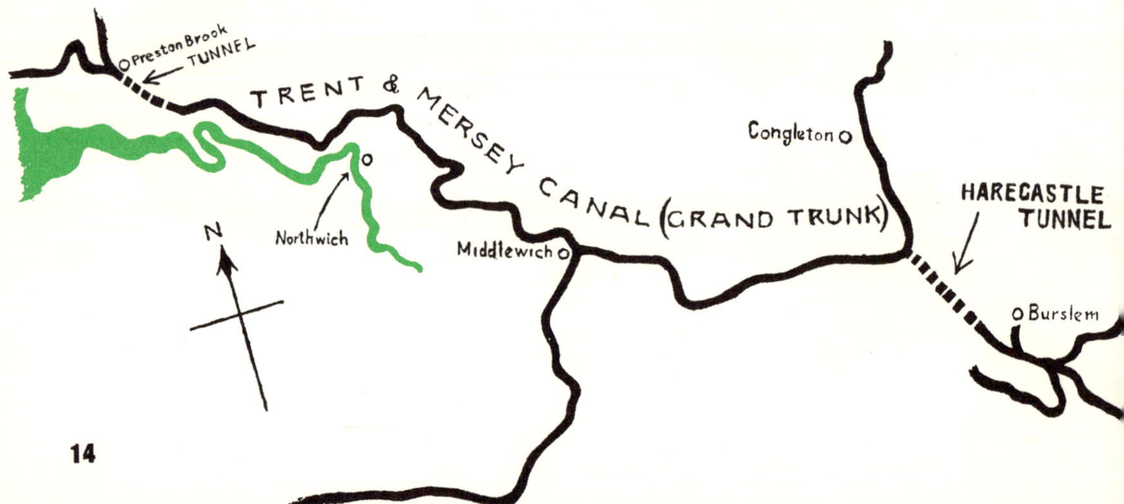

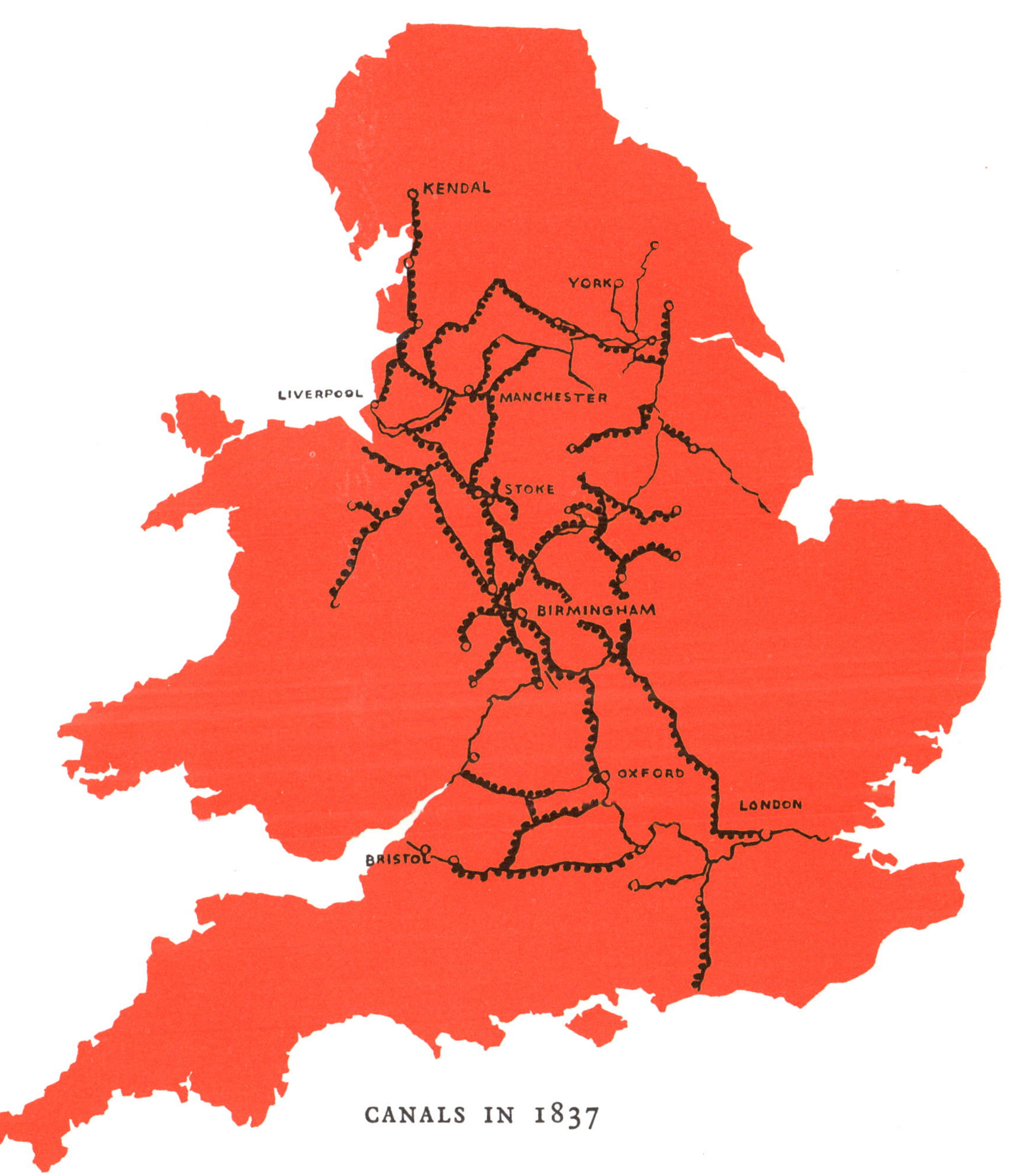

CANALS IN 1837

And then, soon after 1800, the first railways were built.

At first it made little difference to the canals for they were still the cheapest form of transport. In fact, the materials for building railways were carried on the canals. However, as more railways were built the canals were used less.

Railways were faster. People began to think the canals old-fashioned, even though many were improved. As traffic on the canals lessened, the canal companies began to lose money. They were glad to sell the canals to anyone who would buy them. The railway companies bought many to get rid of their rivals, and others closed down. Some were drained and used as routes for new railways.

The great age of canal building was over.

BUILDING THE CANALS

☆ The first canals were almost level. They often followed a valley between two hills. It was cheaper to go round a hill than tunnel through it. Later, when the time taken to carry goods from one place to another became more important, canals were built straighter.

Men who dug out the early canals were called *navigators*, because they planned the direction of the canals. This has given the name "navvy" to men who dig holes. More recent canals were dug out by steam shovels, grabs and dredgers.

A canal is made with sloping sides and a flat bottom. Early canals were lined with puddle clay, a mixture of clay and water. This was put on in many layers, often to a thickness of several feet, making them watertight. Modern canals are lined with concrete.

By the side of most canals is a path called a *towpath*. The first boats were towed or pulled by gangs of men, who walked along the path. Although this was done in some parts of England until 1900, the gangs of men were gradually replaced by horses.

puddle Clay

Sometimes the owners of the land through which the canal passed would not allow a towpath on their side of the canal. Then another one had to be made on the other side. Horses pulling the boat were taken across to the other towpath. Sometimes a bridge was built for this purpose; sometimes the horses were carried across in a special horse-boat.

A canal usually narrows where a bridge crosses it and this is called a *bridge-hole*.

Where a bridge had no towpath running under it, the towrope was cast off the horse as the boat approached the bridge. Then it was refastened at the other side of the bridge.

Tunnels

When a canal had to pass through a hillside, a tunnel was made. Gunpowder was used for blasting and the earth was dug out with picks and shovels, often by candlelight.

If the tunnel was to be a long one, shafts were often sunk from the top of the hill. The earth was then hauled up the shafts. When the tunnel was finished, the shafts were usually covered over, although they were sometimes left uncovered for ventilation.

Most tunnels had no towpath and the boats were *shafted* through. A man stood on the boat and pressed on the roof or sides of the tunnel with a pole or shaft. This pushed the boat along.

Another way of getting the boat through the tunnel was by *legging*. This was done by two men lying on winged boards across the boat and pushing against the wall with their legs. At the longest tunnels there were men who earned their living as "leggers".

In a few early tunnels the boats were pulled through by chains fastened to the walls.

Later, boats which had no engine were towed through the tunnels by steam tugs.

Aqueducts

It is sometimes necessary to carry a canal over a river valley or a stream. Brindley first did this with his canal between Worsley and Manchester by building a bridge called an *aqueduct* to carry the water over the River Irwell.

The first canal engineers built their aqueducts of stone or brick. They lined them with puddle clay so that the water would not leak through. In later aqueducts an iron trough was used.

Locks

In the very early canals, where there was a small hill or a slight slope, a ramp or slipway was built, and the boats were pulled over it.

Some early canals had single gates called *stop-gates* which men raised or lowered by ropes. These were used where the slope of the land was slight. They altered the depth of the water in the canal so that the boats could move up or down the slope.

When a canal is built in hilly country, it must be built in steps, or sections, so the boats can move from one level to another.

The water in each section is held in a basin or *lock*

by gates at each end. This water is used to lift or lower the boats from one section to the next and so move them uphill or downhill.

Locks were not used in Europe until about 1481. Some people claimed that the Dutch were the first to use them, but others said it was the Italians. We know that the Italian painter and sculptor, Leonardo da Vinci, who was also a skilled engineer, built a canal in 1487 and that he used locks.

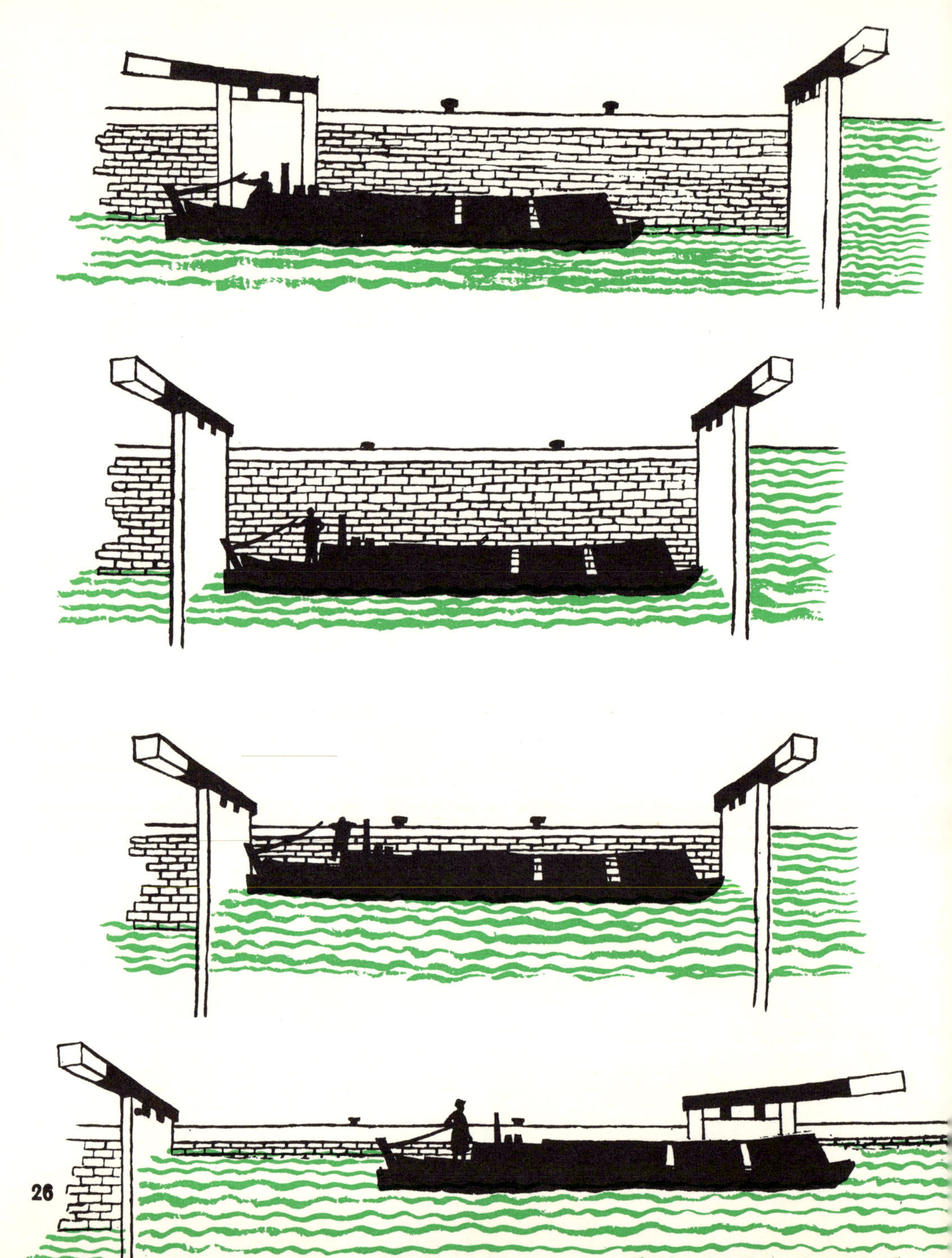

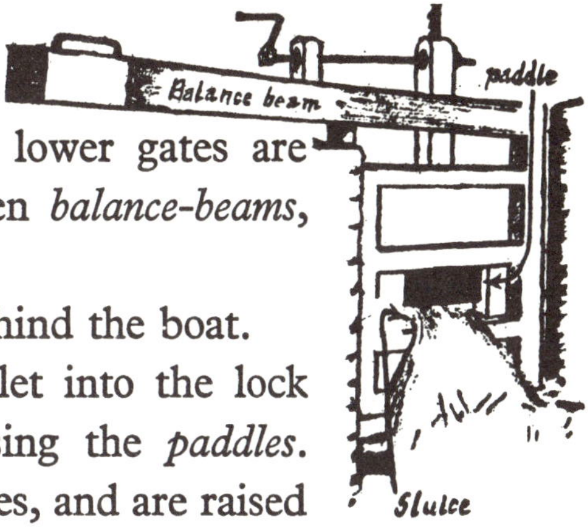

When a boat reaches a lock, the lower gates are opened by pushing the heavy wooden *balance-beams*, and the boat enters the lock.

The lower gates are then closed behind the boat.

Water from the higher section is let into the lock through holes called *sluices*, by raising the *paddles*. These are doors which cover the sluices, and are raised and lowered by a windlass at the top of the gate.

As the lock fills with water, the boat rises with it.

When the boat reaches the level of the water in the next section, the upper gates are opened. The boat is able to pass through into it.

The stretch of water from one lock to the next is called a *pound*.

Water Supplies

A canal must have a plentiful water supply. When a lock is used the water in it runs down to the section below and this water must be replaced. Also in summer time some water is evaporated or dried up by the hot sun.

Water to replace these losses is kept in large lakes called *reservoirs*. It is taken into the canal by narrow channels called *feeders*. Other water is brought from wells, springs and nearby streams.

Sometimes there is a pond by the side of the lock. Then, when the lock is emptied, not quite half of the water goes into the side-pond. When the lock is refilled, the water in the side-pond can be run back into the lock.

Sometimes water is pumped back to the top of the canal.

FEEDER LEADING INTO RESERVOIR

In winter, melting snow and heavy rains fill the canals and so special sluices are built in the sides of the canals to carry away the extra water. When the sluices are opened the surplus water runs over a waterfall called a *weir* and away to the nearest stream.

When the weir cannot take away all the waste water the canal bursts its banks and the water floods out. Extra stop-gates are often built alongside those parts of the canal where this is likely to happen. The damaged part of the canal can then be shut off, preventing further serious flooding of the countryside.

VEIR AT BARROW-UPON-SOAR

THE BOATS ON THE CANALS

☆ The largest number of boats used on Britain's canals were called *narrow boats*. They are seventy feet long and their width, or "beam", is only seven feet. When empty, the hull or bottom of the boat is only nine inches in the water.

Narrow boats usually travelled in pairs. The motor-boat towed the second boat, which was called the *butty*.

The narrow boat was the boatman's home. He was proud of it and made it as attractive as he could. Along the cabin sides were painted patterns in bright colours. Painted roses and castles decorated the cabin doors, water cans and dippers.

Sometimes the cabin chimney was decorated with brasswork.

The butty cabin was only ten feet by six, and the motor-boat cabin was even smaller. Every inch of space was used. The cupboard door let down and became a table. At night the seats became beds and a curtain divided the cabin into two parts. A board was let down from the side to make a further bed across the cabin.

In each cabin a small kitchen range was used for cooking and heating. China plates and polished brasses covered the cabin walls. Later, both boats were fitted with electric lighting.

The cargo was carried in the *hold* of the boat. Sometimes a small part of the hold of the butty boat was used as a general storeroom.

The motor-boat was driven by an 18 h.p. diesel engine which turned the propeller. The engine-room was at the front of the motor-boat's cabin. Each boat was steered by a long-handled *tiller*. The wooden tiller and rudder post of the butty were often bound tightly with white entwined rope as a decoration, known as a *Turk's head*.

PEOPLE ON THE CANALS

☆ In the early days most canal boatmen lived in cottages beside the canals.

Later, when railways began to take trade away from the canals, the boatman was paid less wages. He could no longer afford to pay the rent of a cottage, so he took his family with him on the boat. The boatman's wife helped to steer the boat while the children raced along the towpath to open the heavy lock-gates. It was very hard work, especially in the winter.

Few children could read or write, for they were seldom at school. The boat was never at one place long enough for them to spend more than a few days there and then they would move on.

Nowadays, the goods traffic has gone and very few families live on the boats. But at one time many were born on the boats and lived on them all their lives.

Canal children could attend a school at Southall for a few days when the boats returned to the depot at the end of a trip. The school, which is now closed, was open every day except Sunday and shut for only two weeks in the summer.

A hostel for canal children was opened in Birmingham in 1952. Children lived there while they went to schools nearby. They returned to their parents for the holidays. The hostel is now closed.

FROM LONDON DOCKS TO THE MIDLANDS

At the Depot

☆ The canal boatman's journey began at Bull's Bridge, Southall, which was a British Waterways Depot. The narrow boats were tied up closely together at a long concrete strip called a *lay-by*. Nearby, shipwrights, electricians and carpenters carried out any repairs. There was a paint-shop where the water cans and tillers received their gaily coloured decorations. New ropes, brushes and other equipment were drawn from the large stores. There was a dry dock for any boats needing serious repair.

The boatman collected his trip-card, money and loading orders from the depot offices. He set off to collect his cargo from the warehouses at either Brentford or the Regent's Canal Docks.

At the Docks

The cargo was loaded on to the narrow boats by cranes on the dockside.

Sometimes cargoes were brought up the river by boats called *lighters* which were usually towed by a tug. Other cargoes were brought to Regent's Canal Docks in the ocean-going cargo ships.

When the cargo was safely aboard, the boatman fastened the hold securely. This was called *clothing-up* and protected the cargo from the weather. Some boats had covers made of fibre-glass, which is very light.

Cargoes

Many different cargoes were carried along the canals, some for only short distances, while others made the long journey to the Midlands. Grain was taken to Northampton and Wellingborough, zinc, steel, timber and general cargo to Birmingham.

The boats carried other cargoes on their return journeys. Coal from the Warwickshire collieries, waste materials from the Bourneville chocolate factory and steel tubes from Halesowen were all brought down to factories in the London area. Some cargoes were exported to foreign countries through the Port of London.

On the Journey

The boatman used a thick rope, about 75 feet long, called a *snubber*, for towing the butty behind his motor-boat where locks were a long way apart. Where the locks were close together, or the canal was winding, he used a shorter strap for towing.

Because of heavy traffic, many London locks were built in pairs, side by side, and some were manned by lock-keepers. Further out in the country there was a lock-keeper for a *flight of locks*. This was a number of locks close to each other. At other locks the boatman worked them himself.

At certain places there were checkpoints, known as toll-offices, where the name of the boat, its cargo, destination and time of passing were recorded.

Much time was saved if the locks were open for the boat to enter. Often, one of the boatman's children hurried along the towpath on an old bicycle to the next lock. He told the lock-keeper the boat was coming, or opened the lock-gates himself.

The heavy lock-gates were opened by long wooden beams which acted as levers. The paddles were worked by a windlass usually carried in the boatman's belt. When the boats entered the lock the butty was cast off, brought alongside the motor-boat and tied up to a bollard, known as a *strapping-post*.

After leaving London, the locks took the boats uphill until they reached Tring Summit, the highest point of the journey.

The canal winds on, up and down locks, across aqueducts and through Blisworth and Braunston tunnels. Nearly five days after leaving London the boats reached Birmingham. The boatman had travelled 135 miles and passed through nearly 150 locks.

By rail, the journey from London to Birmingham takes about 2½ hours.

BRITISH CANALS TODAY

☆ After the coming of the railways, few canals were

built, but the opening of the Manchester Ship Canal in 1894 aroused new interest.

Between the two world wars a number of canals were closed, but in 1929 the Grand Union Canal Company was formed from a number of smaller companies. By then, lorry transport was a further rival to the canals.

In 1947 an Act of Parliament called the Transport Act brought most canals under the control of the Dock and Inland Waterways Executive.

Another Act of Parliament in 1953 made further changes. The Docks and the Inland Waterways were separated, and the canals were then run by the British Transport Waterways Division. Since 1963 the canals have been under the control of the British Waterways Board.

SHIP CANALS

☆ Some canals are both deep and wide enough for ocean-going ships.

Ships up to 15,000 tons can travel up the River Mersey and along the Manchester Ship Canal. This canal, which is 36 miles long, has made Manchester an inland port.

The longest ship canal in the world is the Suez Canal, which is 100 miles long. It was built by a Frenchman called de Lesseps about a hundred years ago. It has no locks, but has to be constantly cleared of sand. Ships going through the Suez Canal to India, Australia and the Far East are saved the long journey around Africa.

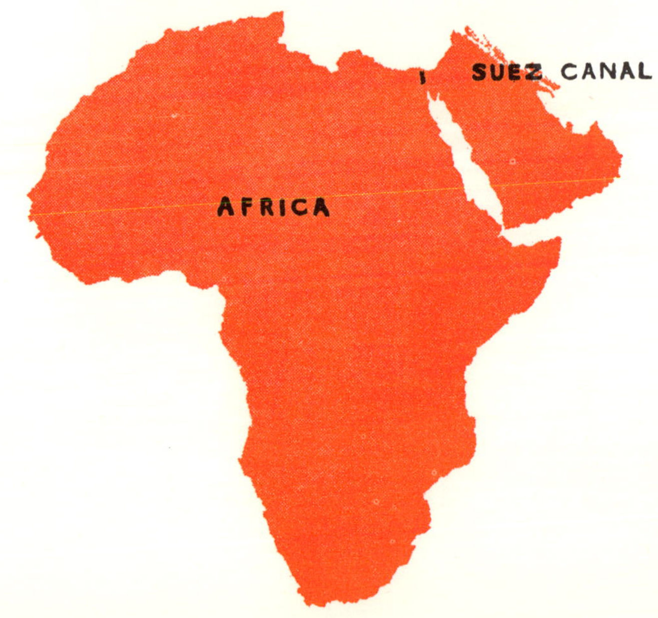

The Panama Canal provides another short cut for ships by joining up the Atlantic and Pacific Oceans. The Panama Canal was difficult to build. The land was swampy and so many men died of malaria and yellow fever that work had to be stopped.

The swamps were breeding grounds for mosquitoes and were sprayed with oil. The mosquito grubs could not breathe through the oil and so were killed. Then it was safe for men to work again.

The Isthmus of Panama is mountainous and rocky. Millions of tons of earth and rock were removed in building the canal.

It takes a ship about two hours to pass through the three huge locks from the Atlantic to the Pacific. The lock gates are the largest in the world. No vessel may steam through the locks for fear of damaging the walls. All ships are towed through by electric engines running on rails beside the locks.

I hope you will make your own book about canals. If you live near a canal, walk along the towpath, look at the boats and watch them go through the locks. Make drawings and models of the boats and locks.

If there is no canal nearby, try to visit the Waterways Museum at Stoke Bruerne in Northants. You will find much helpful information in these books:

INLAND WATERWAYS by Patrick Thornhill, published by Methuen

I-SPY BOATS AND WATERWAYS, published by *Dickens Press*

ROADS AND CANALS IN THE EIGHTEENTH CENTURY by Marjorie Greenwood, published by Longmans

HOW BOATS GO UPHILL by Roger Pilkington, published by Abelard-Schuman

A CANAL TOKEN USED TO PAY LOCK KEEPERS

INDEX